The Three Wishes

and other magical stories

Compiled by Vic Parker

Miles Kelly

First published in 2012 by Miles Kelly Publishing Ltd
Harding's Barn, Bardfield End Green, Thaxted, Essex, CM6 3PX, UK

Copyright © Miles Kelly Publishing Ltd 2011

2 4 6 8 10 9 7 5 3 1

Publishing Director Belinda Gallagher
Creative Director Jo Cowan
Editorial Director Rosie McGuire
Editor Carly Blake
Senior Designer Joe Jones
Editorial Assistant Lauren White
Production Manager Elizabeth Collins
Reprographics Anthony Cambray, Stephan Davis, Jennifer Hunt

All rights reserved. No part of this publication may be reproduced, stored in a retrieval system, or transmitted by any means, electronic, mechanical, photocopying, recording or otherwise, without the prior permission of the copyright holder.

ISBN 978-1-84810-579-9

Printed in China

British Library Cataloguing-in-Publication Data
A catalogue record for this book is available from the British Library

ACKNOWLEDGEMENTS

The publishers would like to thank the following artists who have contributed to this book:
Cover: Peter Cottrill at The Bright Agency
Advocate Art: Alida Massari
The Bright Agency: Marcin Piwowarski, Tom Sperling
Marsela Hajdinjak

All other artwork from the Miles Kelly Artwork Bank

The publishers would like to thank the following sources for the use of their photographs:
Shutterstock: (page decorations) Dragana Francuski Tolimir
Dreamstime: (frames) Gordan

Every effort has been made to acknowledge the source and copyright holder of each picture.
Miles Kelly Publishing apologises for any unintentional errors or omissions.

Made with paper from a sustainable forest
www.mileskelly.net info@mileskelly.net

www.factsforprojects.com

Contents

The Cinder-Maid   4

An Unexpected Opening   16

The Three Wishes   23

Beautiful as the Day   27

The Cinder-Maid

From *Europa's Fairy Book* by Joseph Jacobs

Once upon a time there was a king who had an only son, who was about to come of age. So the king sent round a herald to blow his trumpet and call out, "O yea, O yea, O yea, know ye that His Grace the king will give, on Monday week, a royal ball to which all maidens of noble birth are summoned, and be it furthermore known that at this ball His Highness the prince will select a lady to be his bride. God save the king."

Now there was among the nobles of the king's court one who had married twice. By the first

The Cinder-Maid

marriage he had one daughter. His wife died, and as the girl was growing up her father married again – a lady with two daughters.

His new wife, instead of caring for his first daughter, thought only of her own and favoured them in every way. She would give them beautiful dresses but none to her stepdaughter, who had only to wear the cast-off clothes of the other two. The noble's daughter was set to do all the drudgery of the house, and had nothing to sleep on but the heap of cinders raked out in the scullery, and that is why they called her Cinder-Maid. And no one took pity on her and she would go and weep at her mother's grave where she had planted a hazel tree, under which she sat.

You can imagine how excited everyone was when they heard the herald's proclamation. "What shall we wear, Mother?" cried out the two daughters, and they all began talking about dresses. But when the father suggested that Cinder-Maid should also have

The Cinder-Maid

a dress they all cried out: "What, Cinder-Maid going to the king's ball? Why, look at her, she would only disgrace us all." And so her father held his peace.

Now when the night came for the royal ball Cinder-Maid had to help the two sisters to dress in their fine dresses and saw them drive off in the carriage with her father and their mother. But she went to her own mother's grave and sat beneath the hazel tree and wept. Then a little bird on the tree called out to her:

The Cinder-Maid

Cinder-Maid, Cinder-Maid, shake the tree,
Open the first nut that you see.

So Cinder-Maid shook the tree and the first nut that fell she took up and opened, and what do you think she saw? A beautiful silk dress as blue as the heavens, all embroidered with stars, and two little lovely shoes made of shining copper. And when she had dressed herself the hazel tree opened and from it came a coach all made of copper with four milk-white horses, with coachman and footmen all complete. And as she drove away the little bird called out to her:

Be home, be home ere mid-o'night
Or else again you'll be a fright.

When Cinder-Maid entered the ballroom she was the loveliest of all the ladies, and the prince, who had been dancing with her stepsisters, would dance only with her. But as it came towards midnight Cinder-Maid remembered what the little bird had told her and slipped away to her carriage. And when

The Cinder-Maid

the prince missed her he went to the guards at the palace door and told them to follow the carriage. But Cinder-Maid when she saw this, called out:

Mist behind and light before,
Guide me to my father's door.

And when the prince's soldiers tried to follow her there came such a mist that they couldn't see their hands before their faces. So they couldn't find which way Cinder-Maid went.

When her father and stepmother and two sisters came home after the ball they could talk of nothing but the lovely lady: "Ah, would not you have liked to have been there?" said the sisters to Cinder-Maid as she helped them to take off their fine dresses. "There was a most lovely lady with a dress like the heavens and shoes of bright copper, and the prince would dance with none but her, and when midnight came she disappeared and the prince could not find her. He is going to give a second ball in the hope that she will come again. Perhaps she will not, and

The Cinder-Maid

then we will have our chance."

When the time of the second royal ball came round the same thing happened as before. The sisters teased Cinder-Maid, saying, "Wouldn't you like to come with us?" and drove off again as before. And Cinder-Maid went again to the hazel tree over her mother's grave and cried.

And then the little bird on the tree called out:
Cinder-Maid, Cinder-Maid, shake the tree,
Open the first nut that you see.

But this time she found a dress all golden brown like the earth, embroidered with flowers, and her shoes were made of silver, and when the carriage came from the tree, lo and behold, that was made of silver too, drawn by black horses with trappings all of silver, and the lace on the coachman's and footmen's liveries was also of silver. When Cinder-Maid went to the ball the prince would dance with none but her, and when midnight came round she fled as before. But the prince, hoping to prevent her

The Cinder-Maid

running away, had ordered the soldiers at the foot of the staircase to pour out honey on the stairs so that her shoes would stick in it. But Cinder-Maid leaped from stair to stair and got away just in time, calling out as the soldiers tried to follow her:

Mist behind and light before,
Guide me to my father's door.

And when her sisters got home they told her once more of the beautiful lady that had come in a silver coach and silver shoes and in a dress all embroidered with flowers: "Ah, wouldn't you have liked to have been there?" said they.

Once again the prince gave a ball in the hope that his unknown beauty would come to it. All happened as before – as soon as the sisters had gone Cinder-Maid went to the hazel tree over her mother's grave and wept. And then the little bird appeared and said:

Cinder-Maid, Cinder-Maid, shake the tree,
Open the first nut that you see.

And when she opened the nut, in it was a dress of

The Cinder-Maid

silk as green as the sea with waves upon it, and her shoes this time were made of gold, and when the coach came out of the tree it was also made of gold, with gold trappings for the horses and for the retainers. And as she drove off the little bird from the tree called out:

Be home, be home ere mid-o'night
Or else again you'll be a fright.

Now this time, when Cinder-Maid came to the ball, she was as desirous to dance only with the prince as he with her, and so, when midnight came round, she had forgotten to leave till the clock began to strike, one – two – three – four – five – six, and then she began to run away down the stairs as the clock struck, eight – nine – ten.

But the prince had told his soldiers to put tar upon the lower steps of the stairs, and just as the clock struck eleven her shoes stuck in the tar, and when she jumped to the foot of the stairs one of her golden shoes was left behind. Then the clock struck

The Cinder-Maid

The Cinder-Maid

TWELVE, and the golden coach, with its horses and footmen, disappeared, and the beautiful dress of Cinder-Maid changed again into her ragged clothes and she had to run home with only one golden shoe.

You can imagine how excited the sisters were when they came home and told Cinder-Maid all about it, how the beautiful lady had come in a golden coach in a dress like the sea, with golden shoes, and how all had disappeared at midnight except the golden shoe. "Ah, wouldn't you have liked to have been there?" said they.

Now when the prince found out that he could not keep his lady-love nor trace where she had gone he spoke to his father and showed him the golden shoe, and told him that he would never marry anyone but the maiden who could wear that shoe. So the king, his father, ordered the herald to take round the golden shoe upon a velvet cushion and sound the trumpet and call out: "O yea, O yea, O yea, be it known unto you all that whatsoever lady of noble

birth can fit this shoe upon her foot shall become the bride of His Highness the prince and our future queen. God save the king."

And when the herald came to the house of Cinder-Maid's father the eldest of her two stepsisters tried on the golden shoe. But it was much too small for her, as it was for every other lady that had tried it up to that time. And the herald asked, "Have you no other daughter?"

And the sisters cried out, "No, sir."

But the father said, "Yes, I have another daughter."

And the sisters cried out, "Cinder-Maid, Cinder-Maid, she could not wear that shoe."

But the herald said, "As she is of noble birth she has a right to try the shoe." So the herald went down to the kitchen and found Cinder-Maid, and when she saw her golden shoe she took it from him and put it on her foot, which it fitted exactly. Then she took the other golden shoe from underneath the cinders where she had hidden it and put that on too.

The Cinder-Maid

Then the herald knew that she was the true bride of his master, and he sent for the prince at once.

When the prince saw Cinder-Maid's face, he knew at once that she was the lady of his love. So he took her behind him upon his horse, and as they rode to the palace, the little bird from the hazel tree cried out:

Some squashed their heel, and some squished their toe,
But she sat by the fire who could wear the shoe.

And so they were married and they lived happy ever afterwards.

An Unexpected Opening

An extract from *The Brass Bottle* by F Anstey

Horace Ventimore is a young man living in Victorian times in London. He buys an antique bottle, which turns out to be much more than he had bargained for…

Horace went up to his sitting-room. It was quite dark and he had to light his oil-lamps. After he had done so, the first object he saw was the long-necked jar which he had bought that afternoon, and which stood on the floor near the mantelpiece.

"It's uglier than I thought," he said to himself. "What an idiot I was to waste money on it! I wonder

An Unexpected Opening

if there is anything inside? I'll have to find out before I go to bed."

He grasped it and tried to twist the cap off, but it remained firm, which was not surprising, seeing that it was thickly coated with a crust like cooled, hard lava from a volcano.

"I must get some of that off first, and then try again," he decided, and after foraging downstairs, he returned with a hammer and chisel, with which he chipped away the crust till the line of the cap was revealed, together with a clumsy-looking metal knob that seemed to be a catch. He fiddled with this for some time, and again attempted to wrench off the lid. Then he gripped the vessel between his knees and used all his strength. The cap was beginning to give way, very slightly. One last wrench – and it came off in his hand so suddenly that he fell backwards and hit his head on the floor with a thump.

He had a vague impression of the bottle lying on

An Unexpected Opening

its side, with dense volumes of hissing smoke pouring out of its mouth and towering up in a gigantic column to the ceiling. He was also aware of a strong, perculiar smell, before he fainted clean away.

He could not have been unconscious for more than a few seconds, for when he opened his eyes the room was still thick with smoke. As it cleared, Horace saw the figure of a stranger – an elderly man wearing an Eastern robe and headdress of a dark-green hue. He stood there with uplifted hands, loudly uttering

An Unexpected Opening

something in a strange language. Horace, being still somewhat dazed, felt no surprise. He thought that his landlady must have rented out the next-door apartment at last. His new neighbour must have noticed the smoke and rushed in to offer help.

"Awfully good of you to come in, sir," he said, as he scrambled to his feet. "I don't know what's happened exactly, but there's no harm done. I dare say you've been rather startled. So was I, when I opened that bottle."

"Tell me," pronounced the stranger in a booming voice, "was it thy hand that

An Unexpected Opening

removed the seal, O young man of kindness and good works?"

"I certainly did open it," said Horace, "though I don't know where the kindness comes in – for I've no notion what was inside the thing."

"I was inside it," said the curious stranger, calmly.

"So you were inside that bottle, were you?" said Horace with a smile. "How amazing!" He realised that his new neighbour must be slightly mad, and it would probably be best to play along with him.

"Dost thou doubt that I speak truth? I tell thee that I have been confined in that accursed vessel for countless centuries. Know that he who now addresses thee is Fakrash-el-Aamash, one of the Green Jinn. And I dwelt in the Palace of the Mountain of the Clouds above the City of Babel in the Garden of Irem, which thou doubtless knowest by repute?"

"I fancy I have heard of it," said Horace, as if it were an address in the phone book. "Delightful

An Unexpected Opening

neighbourhood."

"But now, by thy means, my deliverance hath been accomplished. Demand whatever you wish, therefore, and thou shalt receive."

"My dear Mr Fakrash," Horace replied, "I've done nothing – nothing at all – and if I had, I couldn't possibly accept any reward for it."

'Tomorrow,' thought Horace, 'I'll speak to the landlady, and get her to send for a doctor and have this old boy put under proper care – he really isn't fit to live on his own!'

"The hour is late and I will leave thee awhile," proclaimed the stranger. "But I will return and serve you. May thy days be ever fortunate!" And as he finished speaking, he seemed, to Horace's speechless amazement, to slip through the wall behind him. At all events, he had left the room somehow – and Horace found himself alone.

He rubbed the back of his head, which began to be painful. "He can't really have vanished through

An Unexpected Opening

the wall," he said to himself. "I must be over-excited this evening – hardly surprising, with all that has happened. The best thing I can do is to go to bed at once."

Which he accordingly proceeded to do.

The Three Wishes

From *More English Fairy Tales* by Joseph Jacobs

Once upon a time there lived a poor woodman in a great forest, and every day of his life he went out to fell timber. So one day he started out, and his wife filled his wallet and slung his bottle on his back, that he might have meat and drink in the forest. He had marked out a huge old oak, which he could chop into many good planks. When he had reached it, he took his axe and swung it round his head to fell the tree at one stroke. Suddenly, there stood before him a fairy who prayed and beseeched him to spare the tree. He was dazed with

The Three Wishes

wonderment and couldn't open his mouth to utter a word. When he found his tongue at last, he said, "Well, I'll do as you ask."

"Thank you," answered the fairy, "and to show I'm grateful, I'll grant you your next three wishes, be they what they may." With that, the fairy vanished.

The woodman slung his wallet over his shoulder and his bottle at his side, and off he started home. But the way was long, and the poor man was regularly dazed with the wonderful thing that had befallen him, and when he got home there was nothing in his noddle but the wish to sit down and rest. Down he sat by the blazing fire.

"Isn't my supper ready yet?" said he to his wife.

"No, not for a couple of hours," said she.

"Ah!" groaned the woodman. "I wish I'd a good link of black pudding here before me."

No sooner had he said it, when *clatter*, *clatter*,

The Three Wishes

rustle, *rustle*, what should come down the chimney but a link of the very finest black pudding.

"What's all this?" his wife said, gawping in bewilderment.

Then the woodman remembered the fairy and told his wife what had happened.

"Oh, you are a fool," she burst out. "I wish the pudding were on your nose, I do indeed."

Before you could say 'Jack Robinson', there the woodman sat, and his nose was the longer for a link of black pudding.

The Three Wishes

He gave a pull, but it stuck, and she gave a pull, but it stuck, and they both pulled till they had nearly pulled the nose off, but it stuck and stuck.

"What's to be done now?" said he.

"Well… I suppose it doesn't look all that bad," replied his wife.

Then the woodman saw that if he wished, he should wish quickly, and wish he did, that the black pudding might come off his nose. Well! There it lay in a dish on the table, and if the woodman and his wife didn't ride in a golden coach, or dress in silk and satin, why, they had at least as fine a black pudding for their supper as anyone would want.

Beautiful as the Day

An extract from *Five Children and It*
by E Nesbit

*Five children — Cyril, Anthea, Robert, Jane, and the youngest,
a baby whom they call 'the Lamb' — have moved house from
London to the countryside of Kent.*

The children had explored the gardens and the outhouses thoroughly before tea, and they saw quite well that they were certain to be happy at the White House. It was on the edge of a hill, with a wood behind it and the chalk-quarry on one side and the gravel-pit on the other. And it was at the gravel-pit that IT happened…

One day, the children decided to take their

Beautiful as the Day

buckets and spades to dig in the pit, pretending they were at the seaside. They built a big castle, of course. Then Cyril wanted to dig out a cave to play smugglers in, but the others thought it might bury them alive, so it ended in all spades going to work to dig a hole through the castle to Australia. The children dug and they dug and they dug, and their hands got sandy and hot and red, and their faces got damp and shiny. The hole soon grew so deep that Jane begged the others to stop.

"Suppose the bottom gave way suddenly," she said, "and you tumbled out among the Australians, all the sand would get in their eyes."

"Yes," said Robert, "and they would probably hate us, and not let us see the kangaroos, or opossums, or eucalyptus trees, or emus, or anything."

Cyril and Anthea knew that Australia was not quite so near as all that, but they

Beautiful as the Day

agreed to stop using the spades and go on with their hands. This was quite easy, because the sand at the bottom of the hole was soft and fine and dry, like sea-sand. And there were little shells in it.

Nevertheless, Cyril had soon had quite enough. "It's beastly hot in this Australian hole," he puffed. "Let's go and look for bigger shells – I think that little cave looks likely, and I see something sticking out there like a bit of wrecked ship's anchor."

The others agreed, but Anthea carried on digging the hole, because she liked to finish a thing once she had begun it.

The cave was disappointing – there were no shells, and the wrecked ship's anchor turned out to be only the broken end of a pickaxe handle, and the cave party were just making up their minds that the sand makes you

Beautiful as the Day

thirstier when it is not by the seaside, and someone had suggested going home for some lemonade, when Anthea suddenly gave a loud scream:

"Cyril! Come here! Oh, come quick! It's alive! It'll get away! Quick!" They all hurried back to her.

"It's a rat, I shouldn't wonder," said Robert. "Father says they infest old places – and this must be old if the sea was here thousands of years ago."

"Perhaps it is a snake," said Jane, shuddering.

"Oh, don't be silly!" said Anthea. "It's not a rat, it's MUCH bigger. And it's not a snake. It's got feet – I saw them – and fur! And I – it sounds silly, but it said something. It really and truly did."

"What?" Cyril challenged.

"It said, 'You leave me alone'."

But Cyril just observed that his sister must have gone off her nut, and he and Robert dug with spades while Anthea stood on the edge of the hole, jumping up and down. They dug carefully, and presently everyone could see that there really was something

Beautiful as the Day

moving in the bottom of the Australian hole.

Then Anthea cried out, "I'm not afraid. Let me dig," and fell on her knees and began to scratch like a dog does when he has suddenly remembered where it was that he buried his bone.

"Oh, I felt fur," she cried, half laughing and half crying. "I did indeed! I did!" when suddenly a dry husky voice in the sand made them all jump back, and their hearts jumped nearly as fast as they did.

"Leave me alone," it said. And now everyone heard the voice and looked at the others to see if they had too.

"But we want to see you," said Robert bravely.

"I wish you would come out," said Anthea, also taking courage.

"Oh, well – if that's your wish," the voice said, and the sand stirred and spun and scattered, and something brown and furry and fat came rolling out into the hole and all the sand fell off it, and it sat there yawning and rubbing the ends of its eyes with

Beautiful as the Day

its hands.

"I believe I must have dropped asleep," it said, stretching itself.

The children stood round the hole in a ring, looking at the creature they had found. Its eyes were on long horns like a snail's eyes, and it could move them in and out like telescopes. It had ears like a bat's ears, and its tubby body was shaped like a spider's and covered with thick soft fur. Its legs and arms were furry too, and it had hands and feet rather like a monkey's.

"What on earth is it?" Jane said. "Shall we take it home with us?"

The thing turned its strange eyes to look at her,

Beautiful as the Day

and said: "Does she always talk nonsense, or is it only the rubbish on her head that makes her silly?" and it looked scornfully at Jane's hat as it spoke.

"She doesn't mean to be silly," Anthea said gently. "None of us do, whatever you may think! Don't be frightened – we don't want to hurt you, you know."

"Hurt ME!" it said. "ME frightened? Upon my word! Why, you talk as if I were nobody in particular." All its fur stood out like a cat's when it is going to fight.

"Well," said Anthea, still kindly, "perhaps if we knew who you are in particular we could think of something to say that wouldn't make you cross. Everything we've said so far seems to have. Who are you? Don't get angry! Because we really don't know."

"You don't know?" it said. "Well, I knew the world had changed – but – well, really – do you mean to tell me seriously you don't know a Psammead when you see one?"

Beautiful as the Day

"A Sammyadd? That's Greek to me."

"So it is to everyone," said the creature sharply. "Well, in plain English, then, a SAND-FAIRY. Don't you know a Sand-fairy when you see one?"

It looked so grieved and hurt that Jane hastened to say, "Of course I see you are, now. It's quite plain now one comes to look at you."

"You came to look at me, several sentences ago," it said crossly, beginning to curl up again in the sand.

"Oh – don't go away again! Do talk some more," Robert cried. "I didn't know you were a Sand-fairy, but I knew directly I saw you that you were much the wonderfullest thing I'd ever seen."

The Sand-fairy seemed a shade less disagreeable after this.

"It isn't talking I mind," it said, "as long as you're reasonably civil. But I'm not going to make polite conversation for you. If you talk nicely to me, perhaps I'll answer you, and perhaps I won't. Now say something."

Beautiful as the Day

Of course no one could think of anything to say, but at last Robert thought of 'How long have you lived here?' and he said it at once.

"Oh, ages – several thousand years," replied the Psammead.

"Tell us all about it. Do."

"It's all in books."

"You aren't!" Jane said. "Oh, tell us everything you can about yourself! We don't know anything about you, and you are so nice."

The Sand-fairy smoothed his long rat-like whiskers and smiled.

"Do please tell!" said the children all together.

It drew its eyes in and said: "How very sunny it is today – quite like the old times. It used to be very nearly all sand where I lived, and coal grew on the trees, and the periwinkles were as big as tea-trays – you can still find them now, they're turned into stone. We Sand-fairies used to live on the seashore, and the children would come along with their little

Beautiful as the Day

flint-spades and flint-pails, and they would make castles for us to live in. That's thousands of years ago, but I hear that even now children still build castles on the sand. It's difficult to break yourself of a habit."

"But why did you stop living in the sand castles?" asked Robert.

"It's a sad story," said the Psammead gloomily. "It was because they would build moats to the castles, and the nasty wet bubbling sea used to come in, and of course as soon as a Sand-fairy got wet it caught cold, and generally died. And so there got to be fewer and fewer."

"And did YOU get wet?" Robert enquired.

The Sand-fairy shuddered. "Only once," it said. "The very end of the twelfth hair of my top left whisker – I feel the place still if the weather is damp. It was only once, but it was quite more than enough for me."

"I went away as soon as the sun had dried my poor

Beautiful as the Day

dear whisker. I scurried away to the back of the beach, and dug myself a house deep in warm dry sand, and there I've been ever since. And the sea changed its lodgings afterwards. And now I'm not going to tell you another thing."

"Just one more, please," said the children. "Can you give wishes now?"

"Of course," said it, "didn't I give you yours a few minutes ago? You said, 'I wish you'd come out,' and then I did."

"Oh, please, mayn't we have another?"

"Yes, but be quick about it. I'm tired of you."

I daresay you have often thought what you would do if you had three wishes given you, and have despised the old man and his wife in the black-pudding story, and felt certain that if you had the chance you could think of three really useful wishes without a moment's hesitation. These children had often talked this matter over, but, now the chance had suddenly come to them, they could not make

Beautiful as the Day

up their minds.

"Quick," said the Sand-fairy crossly. No one could think of anything, only Anthea did manage to remember a private wish of her own and Jane's which they had never told the boys. She knew the boys would not think much of it – but still it was better than nothing.

"I wish we were all as beautiful as the day," she said in a great hurry.

The children looked at each other, but each could see that the others were not any better-looking than usual. The Psammead pushed out its long eyes, and seemed to be holding its breath and swelling itself out till it was twice as fat and furry as before. Suddenly it let its breath go in a long sigh.

"I'm really afraid I can't manage it," it said apologetically, "I must be out of practice."

The children were horribly disappointed.

"Oh, DO try again!" they said.

"Well," said the Sand-fairy, "the fact is, I was

Beautiful as the Day

keeping back a little strength to give the rest of you your wishes with. If you'll be contented with one wish a day amongst the lot of you I daresay I can screw myself up to it. Do you agree to that?"

"Yes, oh yes!" said Jane and Anthea. The boys nodded. They did not really believe the Sand-fairy could do it.

It stretched out its eyes farther than ever, and swelled and swelled and swelled.

"I do hope it won't hurt itself," said Anthea.

"Or crack its skin," Robert said anxiously.

Everyone was very much relieved when the Sand-fairy, after getting so big that it almost filled up the hole in the sand, suddenly let out its breath and went back to its proper size.

"That's all right," it said, panting heavily. "It'll come easier tomorrow."

"Did it hurt much?" asked Anthea.

"Only my poor whisker, thank you," said he, "but you're a kind and thoughtful child. Good day."

Beautiful as the Day

It scratched suddenly and fiercely with its hands and feet, and disappeared in the sand. Then the children looked at each other, and each child suddenly found itself alone with three perfect strangers, all radiantly beautiful.